R.E.A.L. :
Surprisingly Simple

WAYS TO ENGAGE ADULTS

Loveland, Colorado
group.com

Group resources actually work!

This Group resource incorporates our R.E.A.L. approach to ministry. It reinforces a growing friendship with Jesus, encourages long-term learning, and results in life transformation, because it's

Relational
Learner-to-learner interaction enhances learning and builds Christian friendships.

Experiential
What learners experience through discussion and action sticks with them up to 9 times longer than what they simply hear or read.

Applicable
The aim of Christian education is to equip learners to be both hearers and doers of God's Word.

Learner-based
Learners understand and retain more when the learning process takes into consideration how they learn best.

Surprisingly Simple
WAYS TO ENGAGE ADULTS

Copyright © 2009 Group Publishing, Inc.

Visit our website: **group.com**

Credits
Author: Carl Simmons
Senior Editor: Candace McMahan
Executive Editor: Becki Manni
Chief Creative Officer: Joani Schultz
Copy Editor: Alison Imbriaco
Art Director: Paul Povolni
Designer: Jean Bruns
Cover Designer: Holly Voget
Photographer: Rodney Stewart
Production Manager: Peggy Naylor

ISBN 978-0-7644-3955-1
10 9 8 7 6 5 4 3 2 1   18 17 16 15 14 13 12 11 10 09
Printed in the United States of America.

CONTENTS

IT'S ALL ABOUT
Transformation
5

Going Forward...
TOGETHER
27

IT'S ALL ABOUT
Transformation

Thanks for picking up this little booklet. We'll make it worth your time—because we know you want to make the most of your time with your group or class.

Before we talk about how to make the most of your learning time together, let's talk about what R.E.A.L. is. There's definitely a philosophy here, but don't let that scare you off. Ask yourself these questions right now: How do you believe people learn best in your class or small group? What do you do to make that happen?

Guess what? Your answers are *your* philosophy, whether you think of it that way or not.

So now ask yourself *this* question: How do you know what you're doing is working? To help you think your answer through, ask:

○ Are your group or class members engaged—or glazed?

○ Do people remember what they learned last week? last month? Are they talking about it long after your time together? Are they putting it into practice?

○ And here's the big one: Are they growing in their relationships with Jesus?

We're here to help you with all of these questions. Because R.E.A.L. learning isn't *just* a philosophy—it's a living, active way of learning. It seldom looks exactly the same each time it happens. But it always meets people where they are in their connection with Jesus and helps them get to the next level.

Learning that's R.E.A.L. is

Relational

Experiential

Applicable

Learner-Based

Why does the R.E.A.L. approach work so well in helping people of *any* age learn more about Jesus?

○ **It "sticks."** R.E.A.L. lessons engage people physically and emotionally, as well as verbally. That means there are more "pegs" to hang a memorable lesson on. Lessons have a lasting impact. Research shows that, while most people retain only 5 to 10 percent of what they hear, they retain 80 to 90 percent of what they *experience*. R.E.A.L. lessons lead to high retention.

○ **It gets people talking.** People *will* talk in your group or class when you're using a resource from Group, and that's a good thing. When adults are engaged and excited about learning, they learn more.

○ **It's personalized—*and* it's personal.** We live in a world in which almost anything can be personalized— websites, phones, TV programming, even M&M's! Group resources are personalized, too, because they're learner-based—which means they meet adults wherever they are. However your adults learn, there's something that will work for each person in a Group lesson.

But more important, as adults are engaged and enjoying their time together, and as conversations become more open and honest, the issues the Spirit's been nudging them to deal with will emerge. They'll ask, "How is this lesson applicable to *me*?" We'll give you ideas for putting those heart tugs into action as they happen to create significant, *permanent* life change. If you're not getting excited about making *that* happen, write us. We need to talk.

One more thing: We're not here to tell you that everything you're doing is wrong. It's not. We're here to give you ways to take what you're doing and make it even better, to open up God's message in ways you may never have dreamed of before. And once you've tried the R.E.A.L. approach, your group—and your church—will never be the same.

A CLOSER LOOK

So let's take a close look at each element of the R.E.A.L. philosophy.

It's Relational—You want to help people develop the most important relationship they'll ever have—their relationships with Jesus. And for that matter, you want Jesus to be a part of every other relationship they (and you) have. Our lessons and activities are designed to help you make *all* of that happen. Not only will you help people develop a deeper relationship with Jesus, but you'll also help them participate in discussions that will lead to richer and deeper spiritual friendships with others.

Despite the multitude of virtual connections people have with one another, our society feels lonelier than ever. We have more online friends but fewer flesh-and-blood friends. We all need people we can call on—people we can *count* on. You and your church can be the catalyst for this kind of authentic, genuine friendship, where you can celebrate being the body of Christ together.

And again, people learn better and retain more when they talk than they do when they're being talked *to*. We'll give you great questions to discuss, questions that will allow participants to truly own what they're learning.

It's Experiential—Think about an important, unforgettable life lesson you learned. How did you learn it? Did someone tell you about it? Or did you *experience* it? Most people tell us it's the latter.

And that's why we at Group love to deliver experiences. Again, the more senses we use and the more emotions we engage, the more likely a lesson will *stick*, be unforgettable, and become a part of our daily lives. Jesus knew that. That's why he used everyday items to make *his* messages clear and unforgettable. What's more, experiential learning is a great way to challenge people's assumptions—what they *think* they know—so they can discover God's truth in unexpected ways, even the truths they've heard dozens of times before.

It's Applicable—You're here to help people learn, but more important, you're here to help people grow. That happens when they *use* what they learned. And whether it's with an activity during a lesson or a hands-on take-home assignment, we give people every opportunity to do that—a safe place to experiment, if you will.

Knowledge is good. Putting that knowledge to work in life is far better. As people work through the opportunities we provide, their faith will *become* their lives, and they'll be able to take practical steps toward sharing their lives in Jesus so others can see their faith and respond to it.

It's Learner-based—We measure success not by how much information we present, but by how much people *learn*. Just as important, we measure success by how much of what people know becomes a part of who they *are*. Most people know that the person who learns the most in a teacher-focused class is, well, the teacher. As a teacher or leader, you absorb the material; you wrestle with it; you own it.

How can you help others in your group or class share that sense of ownership? By meeting them right where they are and helping them learn in the ways *they* learn best.

Some people are visual learners—they get it by reading and seeing it. Others are more reflective or "intrapersonal"—they want to share what God's doing, but they need to process what God's doing in *themselves* before they can share it with anyone else. Some are relational and are just champing at the bit to share Jesus with someone else in a meaningful way. Others might be more creative or kinesthetic—they want to not only share their faith, but also do something more physical, tangible, and out-of-the-box with it. However people learn—and however they manifest their faith to others—we'll meet them there.

TAKE A LITTLE TEST

Before we show you how R.E.A.L. learning looks in practice, we'd like you to take a little test. (OK, it's not *exactly* a test. It's actually more like homework. But there *is* a report card involved.) Go to page 30 of this booklet. There you'll find questions about the way you conduct your Sunday school class, teaching, or small group. Work through it in the following order:

○ Rate your response to each statement in the first column. Use a scale of 1 to 5, with 1 meaning the statement is true less than 10 percent of the time and 5 meaning the statement is nearly always true.

○ Sometime in the next week, give everyone in your group a copy of the "Participant's Rating Card," which is on page 31. Go ahead; make copies. Ask people to rate the statements, also on a scale of 1 to 5. Collect their answers, add up the ratings, and divide the total by the number of respondents. Record these averages in the second column of your rating card.

○ Now compare their ratings with yours. What's working? What's not? What are the differences between your impressions and theirs? And why do you think that is? Take the evaluations to heart, and think about what you might be able to do to improve the situation.

○ Then, sometime in the following weeks—and after you've read this booklet—try out some of our suggestions. Afterward, give everyone a new copy of the "Participant's Rating Card," and ask them to rate the statements again. Repeat the process of averaging their comments; then record the averages in the third column of your rating card. Do you see the difference the R.E.A.L. approach makes? We're willing to bet that you'll see immediate, positive changes.

Perhaps you're thinking the R.E.A.L. philosophy sounds great but implementing it would be a stretch for you and your group or class. No worries. We're here to help you with the stretching, too. Read on.

Create an Environment That Invites Learning

If your meeting place *weren't* your meeting place, would you want to hang out there?

If the answer is no, then here are some more questions to ask yourself and members of your group. In what kind of environment would *they* like to learn? To what kind of environment would *they* want to bring their friends? How can your environment help people feel welcome from the moment they walk in?

YOUR MEETING AREA

Stop and take an objective look at your surroundings. Evaluate what your space communicates to others. Ask these questions:

○ **Is everybody comfortable?** Is the temperature at a setting that's not a distraction? Are there enough chairs? Can people sit in them for the duration of your time together without fidgeting?

○ **Is your room the right size?** Is it cramped and a bit stifling? On the other hand, are people way too spread out to connect with one another? Are you in a giant room where it always feels like someone's missing?

○ **Does your meeting area have *any* character?** Is it jazzy and bright? warm and inviting? Or does it feel more like a minimum-security prison? Is there *anything* on the walls? Does your meeting area convey the character and personality of your group, or at least a sense of what they're about to learn and why it's important?

○ **Is the seating arrangement conducive to good discussion?** If everyone's facing forward, change the arrangement. Also change an arrangement that has chairs placed around a long table, which tends to exclude rather than include. Putting people where they can see each other's faces makes for better discussion. Circling your chairs is ideal; you'll get everyone looking at, and relating to, one another instead of only you.

○ **Does your meeting area appeal to all the senses (or at least avoid offending them)?** What would you rather smell: candles, cookies, coffee, or mold? OK, we're pretty sure that last option doesn't appeal to anyone—but you've probably been there, haven't you? And do you *really* want to go back? Again, make your meeting area as inviting as it can be for your particular group.

LIGHTING

Lighting has a direct effect on learning. One study showed that students in classrooms with more natural daylight learn more than 20 percent faster than students with less light.[1] Also, because fluorescent lighting pulses, it creates additional stress and fatigue, especially if there's no source of natural light to help out.

Use natural light if you can, but if you're stuck with fluorescent lighting, use full-spectrum tubes. Your local lighting or hardware dealer will be able to help you find them.

While you're evaluating the lighting in the room you'll use, also consider how bright it is. Think about your favorite restaurant or coffee shop; now compare it with a fast-food restaurant, where the lighting is bright and harsh. Subdued lighting is more conducive to deep conversation than bright light.

SOUND

Music has repeatedly been proven to enhance learning. Music and long-term memory are both tied to the part of the brain that's responsible for many of our emotions—so take advantage of that. The specific style of the music isn't critical, as long it's background music rather than foreground music. Soft jazz, classical, or other instrumental music will work. Music not only enhances your learning environment but can be a powerful mood setter. Use music to open your group's minds *and* hearts to what the Spirit wants to communicate.

So your meeting area is ready. Are *you*? Read on.

---

1. Study conducted by California Board for Energy Efficiency and Pacific Gas and Electric, cited in *The Accelerated Learning Handbook* by Dave Meier (New York: McGraw-Hill, 2000) 170.

Get Ready—It's Easy

PREPARING YOUR LESSON

You're busy. So we're careful to keep your prep time to a minimum. To set up, lead, and debrief a lesson successfully, follow these simple steps:

○ **Highlight the questions you feel are especially important.** We know you enjoy setting your group up for "aha" moments. You'll be having a good discussion or debriefing an activity, and wham! *That* question—the one that addresses the "elephant in the room"—pops up. And when that happens, so does life change. You'll want to be ready for that moment. R.E.A.L. learning gives you permission to go where the Spirit leads rather than feel you need to "stick to the lesson."

○ **Have supplies on hand.** We keep the number and complexity of supplies to a minimum (and some lessons are even "prop-free"). But be sure to check your materials and gather supplies beforehand.

○ **Preview and cue film clips.** We'll talk about the value of film later, but if you do use film clips in your lessons, cue them up, set the volume, and test the equipment before people arrive.

Never assume that everyone has seen the film you're using. Also, watch the scene suggested in the lesson first and make sure you understand the beginning and ending cues. If your DVD player has a subtitle function, and you have a larger class or group, consider turning it on so that people can follow any dialogue they might miss otherwise.

You can estimate the number of people who can comfortably see a television screen by measuring the screen's width. For example, a 23-inch screen works for 20 to 25 people.

○ **Get others involved.** Don't be afraid to ask for volunteers. They can lighten your load. Who knows? People may want to commit to teaching a lesson, bringing the snack, or hosting—and as they do, they'll discover more about how God has built *them*.

Most important...

PREPARE *YOURSELF*

If you like a good conversation, you'll thrive in a R.E.A.L. learning environment from the get-go. If not, that's OK. We've created our lessons so anyone can lead them. The important thing is that you trust us here.

Our chief creative officer, Joani Schultz, has an adage about leading people into R.E.A.L. experiences:

> "If *you* believe they'll do it, they *will*."

Don't apologize for other people's potential discomfort. Don't cut things out because you don't know if they'll "get" it. And *don't* go on about your own reservations about an activity, if you have any. Just do it. Then watch what happens. Believe God will work!

And if an activity flops, so what? It happens. You've probably had plenty of by-the-book discussions that have left people asking "Huh?" or just staring blankly at you. So give yourself permission to experiment, play, and maybe even fail on occasion. If you do fail, have a good laugh, and move on. The upside is so much greater than any perceived discomfort you might feel. You *want* to push people out of their comfort zones so God can teach them something brand-new. So take the leap, and trust God.

God doesn't mind pushing us out of our comfort zones so we can grow closer to him. You see God doing that with every important person in the Bible: Noah, Abraham, Moses, Joseph, Esther, David,

Peter, the other disciples…the list goes on. Think about the times God has changed *you*. More than likely, God first had to pull you out of your comfort zone to do it.

One more thing: Pray. A lot. Pray for yourself, and pray for your group members. Ultimately, everything we at Group do is only table setting for what God wants to do with your class or group. So spend some time inviting God into your group time. And watch what happens.

Make Learning Unforgettable

FIRST THINGS FIRST

Welcome everyone.

That's obvious, right? But honestly, how often do we get so caught up in logistics that we fail to engage the very people we want to see grow in Jesus?

So again: Welcome everyone. If you can't be at the door or your group is too large for individual welcomes to be practical, be sure to welcome everyone as a group. Say something like "I'm really glad you all made it here today. Every one of you is important to this group. Today we're going to focus on…" If it's appropriate, mention last week's study to bring everyone up to date.

You want people to open up. You want them to hear about Jesus. But more than likely, they aren't going to do either if they feel uncomfortable, left out, or ignored. The experience people have with you often mirrors the experience they'll have with God. So if every part of your time together is welcoming, they'll treasure it and want more of it—just as they'll want more of Jesus.

OPENING EXPERIENCES

The people you're welcoming may have just finished a busy day at work or had a hectic drive to church on a Sunday morning. That's why we design opening experiences to give everyone a 5- to 10-minute transition time to unwind before diving into each lesson.

An opening experience might include a snack or a movie clip; it might be an activity; it might just be an opportunity to talk in a group of two or three. Whatever it is, it prepares people to dig deep into the lesson. And more than likely—because they're having such a good time doing it—they won't even realize that they've *already* started the lesson!

From there, things can go in any number of directions. And that's a good thing. The element of surprise is your friend, not your enemy. Like C.S. Lewis' famed lion, Aslan, R.E.A.L. learning isn't tame, but it's good.

So in that spirit, let's drill into an area you're almost certainly familiar with —and discover how the R.E.A.L. approach makes learning different.

R.E.A.L. BIBLE EXPLORATION

Many of Group's lessons include at least one question that calls for multiple Scripture references to be divided among your group members, so everyone explores a section and reports back to the entire group. Exploring Scripture this way has several important purposes: It saves time, it engages everyone, and it leads to insights you would never have thought of otherwise (because, well, someone else *did* think of them).

Our questions aren't your normal, fill-in-the-blank Bible study questions. It's good to know facts about Scripture. It's even better to understand what a given passage says. It's better yet to understand what God wants to show you and your group and what God wants each of you to do with that understanding. To help people reach this level of understanding, our questions are surprising, specific, and personal. As you use these questions, you'll see God's Word in a way you never have before.

INTERACTIVE EXPERIENCES

When we talk about experiences, we're talking about activities that require everyone to participate somehow, not just sit back and listen. The experiences might be fun, meditative, or even uncomfortable—but the end result is that the experiences engage everyone. From each unforgettable experience, you'll build a bridge to an unforgettable truth. (We'll get into that more in "Set Up Great Discussions.")

Don't be afraid to experiment, and don't be afraid to invite everyone to "play along." This invitation gives people permission to be uncomfortable, but also tells them they're not going to get an "out." When you tell them to play instead of "work," you're giving them permission to get whatever God wants *them* to get out of the activity, rather than creating expectations they can't (and possibly don't want to) live up to.

FILM

Film is a powerful storytelling medium. In that sense, it can function a lot like Jesus' parables—it can set us up to hear a truth we weren't prepared to hear. And by doing so, it can flesh out biblical truths in a fresh, new way. Film also provides a safe entry to what could become a much heavier and more personal discussion. It's often easier to react to something you're seeing in a film clip than to a direct question. But once you've reacted, you're in.

Again, make sure you've previewed any clips before you show them, so you're ready and comfortable using them (and the technology) during your meeting.

MUSIC

Group's R.E.A.L. experiences might also include certain pieces of music. Because music can evoke deep emotion, it can be a catalyst to a great discussion. And like film clips, music can ease people into the deep end without their even knowing it.

WHEN TO CUT, HOW TO CUT, AND WHEN NOT TO CUT

You might be thinking, "Wow, that's a lot to pack into a lesson." We know. We understand the issue of time limitations, and we construct our lessons with those time frames in mind. Still, a great experience or question might start a great discussion that you don't want to cut off. Or someone might really open up, and you're not about to get in the way of the Spirit's movement in his or her life. Then what?

When that happens, feel free to trim the lesson *anywhere*.

On the other hand, permission to trim the lesson is not permission to skip an activity because it makes you uncomfortable. The more senses and learning styles you engage, the more these lessons stick. So as tempting as it might be to "cut to the message" or the group interaction, it's always better to lead people into an experience they'll never forget. If you do skip sections of the lessons, here are a few suggestions:

○ Cut from the middle, rather than the beginning or the end.

○ Never cut an experience in favor of leader talk.

○ And here's another, even better alternative: If you're not tied to a clock or a calendar, use as much time as it takes to get through a lesson. If you need another half-hour or another week, take it. Understanding what God wants to tell your group is *always* more important than "covering the material" or staying within a given time frame. Let God do what he wants to do, and give him the time to do it fully.

Set Up Great Discussions

We love a great discussion, and we suspect you do, too—even if you're not used to having one during a lesson.

As a discussion takes on a life of its own, though, you can't be sure where it's headed. That's the wonder of it. But lack of direction can be a bad thing, too. So let's talk about how to make your discussions as meaningful as possible.

THE IMPORTANCE OF GOOD QUESTIONS

As we've mentioned, our questions aren't your typical Bible study questions. We want you to think about what you believe, why you believe it, and how your life can be different *because* you believe it. Therefore, we ask questions that are

○ **surprising**—You'll move past biblical facts and into seeing God's Word in a way you never have before. If our questions don't accomplish that, we've failed.

○ **specific**—General biblical truths are good, and sometimes it's necessary to reiterate them. Getting at what the Bible really says about the topic you're studying, and how it applies to us now, is even more important. Which brings us to...

○ **personal**—We want you to understand not only what God is saying, but also what God's saying to each individual. So we'll ask the hard questions. The discomfort people feel as they struggle to answer these questions? It's called growth. But the good news is: You and your group are in this together. And as you bring the real issues out, God will grow all of you, together. Transparency breeds transparency, and growth breeds more growth.

One more thing: In order to make our questions surprising, personal, and specific, we also make sure they're open-ended. Nothing kills a discussion faster than a yes-or-no or fill-in-the-blank question, so you won't find them in our lessons. Open-ended questions demand more than a quick nod. They demand that people respond to what God is trying to teach them. And when they do, great discussions happen.

RESPONDING THOUGHTFULLY

Not every great question is in the lesson, however. In fact, as much as we like our questions, the most important questions you'll address may well be the ones your group comes up with as they dig in. Here are some suggestions for dealing with them:

- ○ **Be prepared.** If you've taken the time to digest the lesson beforehand, you'll have your own responses to share, and you'll be ready to ask others about theirs.

- ○ **Push beyond rote "Sunday school" answers to get at what people *really* mean.** This could be as simple as asking, "Could you explain that a little more?" or just saying, "Say more." Even if they stumble a bit as they think it through, continue to encourage them to articulate what they're thinking. Chances are, someone else is thinking the same thing.

- ○ **Be careful how you respond.** Sometimes you'll get answers that you (and probably others in the group) *know* aren't biblically accurate. You don't want to misrepresent God's truth, but you don't want to misrepresent God's love, either. Acknowledge all answers, so people realize that *every* response is important. Say something like "Thank you" or "That's an interesting observation." If necessary, address the comment right then and there; otherwise, look for an opportunity to discuss it with that person after your meeting.

○ **Restate what you think you're hearing.** Say something like "If I'm understanding correctly, you're saying…" As you help people work through their own thoughts, you'll help them reach deeper understandings or discover contradictions in their beliefs they might not have even been aware of.

○ **Open up the discussion.** Say something like "Who has something to add to what _____ is saying?" This keeps discussion going and prevents one participant from dominating the discussion.

○ **Try not to have the first or last word on every question** (or even most of them). Give everyone the opportunity to participate. At the same time, don't put anyone on the spot. Remind people that they don't have to answer any questions they're not comfortable answering. You want your group or class to be a safe place where people feel free to share their thoughts and struggles. Many people aren't used to this kind of learning environment, so the tone you set will make the difference between rich conversation, and having real faith issues and questions kept "off the table."

DEEPENING DISCUSSIONS

Pair Shares and Subgroups

We often suggest that groups form pairs or smaller groups (usually between three to five people). It may feel risky. Perhaps you've never led a group this way before, or you think people have come to hear you teach, not to talk to each other. And what if nobody says anything?

Relax. It's a little riskier, but it's also more rewarding. So be sure to take advantage of using pair shares and subgroups when we suggest them. Here are some reasons:

○ The larger your group, the more challenging it is to get

everyone to participate. Using pairs and subgroups eliminates the problem of one or two people dominating the discussion.

○ Participation and learning increase when everyone's involved. And because of that, the possibility of life change increases, too.

○ Subgroups provide a great opportunity for you to show confidence in your other potential leaders. What better way to develop leadership in another person than by giving him or her a hands-on opportunity to lead?

○ It's an efficient use of your time. You'll be able to explore Bible passages, experiences, and questions in a timelier manner using twos or threes.

○ And perhaps most important, a pair or subgroup helps people express their own struggles and questions in an environment that's not as intimidating as a larger group. In smaller groups, they can be both honestly critiqued and wholeheartedly encouraged. And when that happens, growth happens.

You can rotate the makeup of your pairs or subgroups, have groups form randomly, or keep them the same each week. Do whatever you think works best for your group.

Debriefing

As you work through our lessons, people won't just answer questions; they'll debrief and discuss what they learned and how they learned it. Debriefing can happen after an experience, after a Bible discussion, or after a pair-share or subgroup discussion. If people were working in small groups or pairs, bring everyone together to talk about what just happened. As people discuss what they were *really* thinking and feeling, they'll gain a far deeper understanding of what God is revealing to them.

Debriefing is one of the most critical parts of R.E.A.L. learning. We think it's so important that some of our studies spend entire sessions debriefing a shared experience. When people are given the chance to process what they've learned together, they're far more likely to remember it long after they leave and to incorporate those aha moments into their daily lives. So make the most of your time together. Talk about it. Learn from it. Take it with you when you go.

WHEN IS IT GOING DEEPER AND WHEN IS IT A RABBIT TRAIL?

One hallmark of a great discussion is that you're not entirely sure where it's headed. But another hallmark is that it ultimately arrives at the destination God has in mind.

So how can you tell when a discussion is really going deeper (even if it's taking an unusual route to get there), and when it's just going nowhere (or somewhere it really *shouldn't* be going)? Here are a couple of questions to keep in mind:

- ○ Is this discussion really connected to the theme of the lesson?

- ○ More important, is this discussion helping group members draw closer to Jesus?

One caveat: Sometimes the answer to the first question is no, even while the answer to the second is yes. This usually happens when someone in your group is having a breakthrough (even if it might look like a break*down* to some). It's clear that God is doing some serious work in the person's life, although that work might be totally unrelated to the theme of the lesson.

When that happens, pull over, and deal with it as a group. God moments should always, *always* take precedence over "covering the material."

But if the answer to both questions is no, it's time to move on. Here are some techniques that can help you keep your group on track:

○ Give your discussion a time limit, and give everyone a one- or two-minute warning before time is up.

○ If someone's dominating the conversation or taking it down the wrong path, kick it back to the rest of the group. Say something like "Who has something to add to what _____ is saying?" or "How can we tie this to the subject of _____?"

○ Or you can simply say, "OK, everyone, let's reel it back in now." That comment usually gets a good laugh, but everyone gets the point.

○ And there's always that old grade-school standby of raising your hand until everyone stops talking. But use this one as a last resort.

Move From Understanding to Growing

PUTTING FAITH INTO ACTION

You've almost finished the lesson (and for that matter, this booklet). You've all had a good time together. People have learned more about God's Word and what God wants them to do with what they learned.

So it must be time to go home, forget everything you've learned together, and come back to learn something entirely new next week, right?

C'mon, you *know* the right answer.

And yet that scenario is played out in millions of Christian lives every week, in Sunday schools and small groups all over the world.

We'd like to change that, and we're thinking you'd like to as well. (Would you have gotten this far if you *didn't*?)

So let's talk about how you and your group will move from understanding how what you've been studying applies to your lives to considering ways to get out there and really *apply* it.

In nearly every lesson we offer, we provide practical, doable take-home ideas that people can do either individually or as a group—so that what they've learned becomes R.E.A.L. in their own lives.

Again, different people learn in different ways. Furthermore, some people need baby steps, and some are ready to take giant leaps. The options we offer reflect these differences. Some need to read and process; others are ready to get their hands dirty; others want to get together with a friend and share everything God's showing them *right now*. However they're built, we'll provide practical ways for people to apply what they've learned.

So don't let your group off the hook. Encourage people to do the assignments we offer. Encourage them to talk to at least one other person in the group about what they're doing, either during the week or during your next meeting. Accountability is a powerful thing. Take advantage of it.

PLUGGING INTO THE ULTIMATE POWER SOURCE: PRAYER

We often suggest that you end your time together in prayer, and we'll usually provide suggestions for how to do that, from simply asking God to help you remember and live out the lesson to a full-blown prayer experience that will help the message stick even more.

But it's your class or group, so ultimately you need to do what works best. Here are some general suggestions to make your prayer time more effective and powerful:

○ Don't assume that people will be comfortable praying out loud, especially if it's your first time together.

○ Be careful not to call on someone to pray out loud unless you know ahead of time that he or she is comfortable doing so or have asked beforehand.

○ In a first meeting in which people may not know each other well, ask for prayer requests, and then offer a closing prayer yourself. To solicit prayer requests, simply ask, "How can this group pray for you this week?"

○ Consider forming pairs or small groups for prayer. People are more likely to share personal requests in a more intimate setting. They may feel comfortable telling what they need prayer for and more comfortable offering silent prayer for their partners. You know your group's makeup best.

○ Ask everyone to complete a simple one-sentence prayer. For example, "Lord, I want to thank you for…" or "Lord, help me to become closer to you in…"

○ Don't overlook the power of silent prayer. The fact that you're not hearing it doesn't mean God's not listening.

○ Pray Scripture together. The Lord's Prayer and selected psalms are good examples of Scripture to pray. The group might read the entire passage together, or people might read smaller portions of it individually. Praying Scripture may make it easier for your "non-pray-ers" to pray aloud.

○ Ask everyone to "pray for the person to your right or left— silently or aloud." Ask people who pray silently to say "amen" at the end of the prayer to indicate that they have finished.

○ Don't solicit prayer requests beforehand. Just allow everyone to pray. If something needs clarification, you can always discuss it afterward (and maybe even pray more, if you have the opportunity).

The single most important thing a leader can do for his or her group is to spend time in prayer for group members. So why not take a minute to pray for your group right now?

Going Forward...
TOGETHER

R.E.A.L. learning doesn't end when the lesson is over. So be ready to take any or all of the following actions:

○ **Clarify sessions' ending times.** People may want to hang out and talk after your official meeting time. If for any reason you need people to leave by a certain time, be sure to make this clear before or during your session. Otherwise, be there for your group as much as possible. It may very well turn out that someone wants to discuss something important but didn't feel comfortable bringing it up during your meeting time.

○ **Follow up.** If someone in the group has faced a big issue during the week, be sure to follow up with a call, card, visit, or e-mail.

○ **Suggest during-the-week connections.** Encourage people to touch base with one another during the week. They might talk about how they're doing with the take-home assignment. Or they might just encourage each other. The healthier a group is, the more likely it is that the real ministry is taking place *between* your meeting times.

○ **Evaluate.** As leader, take a minute to think about how things went. And since we've mentioned that, did you start your report card? (If you haven't, it's on page 30. The rating card for group members is on page 31.) If you've given R.E.A.L. learning a try, it's time to ask your group to fill out the rating

card again. After you've averaged the responses, fill in the
third column on your rating card. How did you do?

And hey, how did *we* do? We're your partner and friend in ministry,
after all. So keep us posted.

Which brings us to this: Let us know about your successes. Let us
know what we can do better and how we can help you more. If there's
an area you'd like us to address in future resources, tell us that,
too. Write us at Group Publishing, Inc., P.O. Box 481, Loveland,
Colorado 80539, or send an e-mail to info@grouppublishing.com.
We'd love to hear what you're thinking. (Yes—*really!*)

> May God bless you and your group on your
> journey together. And as God takes you to all the
> places and experiences he has for each of you,
> never forget: You're all in this together. You,
> God, and everyone he puts in your path. And
> nothing is more R.E.A.L. than that.

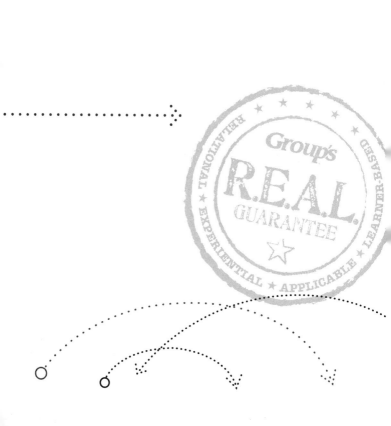

LEADER'S RATING CARD

Rate the following statements on a scale of 1 (the statement is true less than 10 percent of the time) to 5 (the statement is true nearly all the time).

	Leader's rating *before* R.E.A.L.	Participant's rating *before* R.E.A.L.	Participant's rating *after* R.E.A.L.
Anyone entering our meeting area for the first time feels welcome.			
We not only learn together, but also enjoy meeting together.			
We get into great discussions about what we're learning.			
Everyone in our group is engaged with the lesson, even those who are not great talkers.			
We all understand the relevance of what we're learning in our own lives.			
People are not only learning more about their faith, but also putting what they're learning into practice.			
People remember the lesson and what it meant to them for at least a week.			
Our friendships with one another are growing because of our time together.			
People are growing in friendship with Jesus because of our time together.			
People are becoming more like Jesus because of our time together.			

PARTICIPANT'S RATING CARD

Rate the following statements on a scale of 1 (the statement is true less than 10 percent of the time) to 5 (the statement is true nearly all the time).

	Your rating
Anyone entering our meeting area for the first time feels welcome.	
We not only learn together, but also enjoy meeting together.	
We get into great discussions about what we're learning.	
All the people in our group are engaged with the lesson, even if they're not great talkers.	
We all understand how what we're learning applies to our own lives.	
Not only are we learning more about our faith, but we're also putting what we're learning into practice.	
We remember the lesson and what it meant to us for at least a week.	
Our friendships with one another are growing because of our time together.	
We're growing in friendship with Jesus because of our time together.	
We're becoming more like Jesus because of our time together.